T5-AGP-805

The Square Root of Female

Gillean Chase

1984

ISBN 0-920304-35-4

Book Cover Illustration: Wendy Frith
Design: Cape Traverse Associates
Typesetting: McCurdy Printing & Typesetting
Printing: Les Editions Marquis Ltée

With thanks to the Canada Council for its support

Ragweed Press
Charlottetown, P. E. I.
C1A 7N7

Canadian Cataloguing in Publication Data

Chase, Gillean, 1946-
The square root of female

POEMS. ISBN 0-920304-35-4

I. Title.

PS8555.H39S69 1984 C811'.54 C84-099374-9
PR.9199.3.C447S69' 1984

This book is dedicated to the Muses, and to the life force which opens my senses. In a concrete way,it is also dedicated to the women in my life whose strength and integrity inspire me.

Contents

night of the novenas

I

i reach to take the pulse of the moon
and find it shuddering
cold sweat drips from its dim face
beading into the aurora borealis.

do not walk by the shore
tonight do not watch the dawn
your feet will be lashed by the sharpened
spines of dead fish
ancient crustaceans will reach
snapping

drag you
gill-less shell-less
collapse your temples
and scatter your novenas

isis preserve you child
to worship the moon is mad

i am recent
history dredged me gulping
from the amniotic ocean
mutant lungs
struggling to expand
in this frog's element.

breathing became my first prayer
survival and fear the basis
of my gods.

II

women who bleed
women who labour
women who squat
parallel
that terrible first progeny
repeat and repeat the mutation
until all of us are driven
from the ocean's womb:
   expelled
   unto the lap of land
   exiled to the uncertain
   milk of mountains.

now only the moon
claims us blood and gristle
draws us through the nights
of dying stars towards her
pale and waning face.

great isis you shall not let us go
although all the gods of earth
struggle to keep us from your womb.

we are drawn always
to the lures:
after birth the umbilical cord
curves like a hook in our bellies.

Forty Days of Rain

Forty days of rain
and still no sign of Noah
the ark elusive.
Animals will not pair
these days
nor lie down
quiescent with lions.
The snake is writhing
restless with cold
and will not circle
the hilt of the healing sword.

Physicians cannot cure.
They engage in delicate debate
with spider crab or rock
lobster, eyes submerged.

Along the San Andreas fault
anticipatory trembling
delicious
as the first kiss of lovers.
Mount St. Helens adds heat
to the computations of scholars.
Parthenogenetic virgin
she spews forth
the terrible toothless infant
of our human discontent.

Forty days of rain
and far too many years
outside Eden
prophets sell expedient solutions
to leaders surfeited on holocaust.
Insurance salesmen
stock up on rat poison
and scurry away from sounds
in the walls.

The eyes of the hungry blink.
Like amphibious fish they are
learning to use their thin lungs.

Swan Song

Tonight sucks the ovaries
like the rattler sucks eggs.

Plumage of the mystic bird
god fallen upon Leda
union of feathers and flesh.

Your toes are clawed.
Strong beak descends to my breast.
You poise between passage and return.

I am rite of sacrifice
or meat for carrion crow
God of terror.
Tenderness is not legion
this act beyond rape or love.

I am expelled
my womb heaves:
die
to be born
to be borne
up

tossing vomit into the sea.

A Vision from the Bentall Tower

Viewed from the twenty-seventh floor
of the Bentall Tower
arms and legs propel bodies
jerky squid motions
in some thin atmosphere
we call air

From even farther up
one can imagine how we look
skins clinging to us
like brittle shells
submerged in a gaseous green
and red-rimmed world
hollowed out offices waving
at the landscape like sea
algae quivering

The earth will swallow
take us beneath
what we used to call
the bottom floor
our fingers
reaching for the ejector button

What other world is there
besides the dread tide which is Now
bearing us forward—
survival to be rediscovered
like Atlantis
or other buried continents
beneath layers of obsidian
conchoidal fractures of intelligence
and faith

One suffers from vertigo
or the bends
from the twenty-seventh floor
of the Bentall Tower

The Late, Last Paradise

There is in man
an amazing desire
to defecate:
the oceans run with effluvient
large and hideous deformities
are pulled from the rivers and bays.

Sewers are reaching out
encompassing even the exotic
distant islands
where simple natives
are said to dissport themselves
free of western inhibitions.
The missionary position
I am told is never used there.

I repeat. There is in man
an amazing desire
to explore
—"going where no man
has ever gone before"—
pushing back the boundaries of space
like foreskin circumcised
savagery turned
to the use of civilization.

In the search for new frontiers
space is becoming the next
lavoratory. Columbia's payload
servicing the free world
trajectory
pointed towards the belly
of the Russian bear.
The woods are no longer big enough
or leaves in the hand
to wipe the ass
of capital clean.

Restraint, Freud intones
is the first act of human culture.
Society based upon the collective
agreement to postpone pleasure
defer gratification.
This leads to massive problems
with the sphincter muscles
of humankind.

Note the shape of bombs
or missiles
steaming turds
intended to burst
on contact with the ground.

Wars happen
because man is frustrated
by concentrating on proper toilet
training.
When what he really wants
is to "let 'er rip."
There's a playground out there after all:
earth and ocean
air and countless places
which prevent us
from noticing the stinking
flesh of our late, our last paradise.

Ask the Dolphins

What do dolphins know
who have watched the ships of men
belching
or drifted beyond the flotsam
of battered rigs
grey mornings after
the ocean has swallowed?

Oceanid churns out her litany in waves:
for fishes dead for algae
fatal effluents
spotting her intestinal tract.
She vomits man's chemical Chimaera
to rid herself of it.

> What do dolphins know
> unless their dreams are beginning
> to be polluted
> hallucinogenic fantasies of mass
> extinction
> : the earth reaching out for them
> like Hitler's ovens
> green gas
> lifted by the breeze.

Perhaps their eyes are burning
acid smart that drives them
floundering to the breakers
to suicide. Obliterating
their natural memory
of the boy who rode the backs
of so many dolphins.

The Dream

I sit astride a wooden pier
deteriorated by long disuse.
Wooden sticks tied together
by ancient rope lean above
a grey mirror surface.
My legs and arms are reflected from an angle
curious.

A black boat lies overturned.
Old skiffs float
adrift in shallows.

I might leap from the wobbly pier
into soft
dirty sand
an inch short of my ankles.

Seated I defy the law of gravity
the laws of stress and balance.
Thoughts ripple
from the black dory
in telepathic waves.
I am struck, mid-brow
—message of things abandoned.
Caution is crucial.

Slowly the companion
skiffs turn true to an idle current.
Even their oarlocks
are long-since rotted.

Perched on the pier like a black crow
another figure speaks:
indistinguishable
words and gender.
I receive at the temple
in the same cerebral way.
Soundless warning.

In the grey mud dawn
I remember: wood
takes a long time to rot
even in water.

Ritual

Hair skin cartilage
the line of jaw and brow protruding
towards this particular day.

In the nighttime
her image disappears.
Morning she reassembles it
familiarizes herself
with her changling face.

In sleep she is no more
than organs of maintenance:
heart lungs
a brain
throwing off energy in images
she strains to recall.

The mirror captures her.
Riding like a continental plate
her personal history grinds:
the warp begins around
mouth and eyes.

With morning ablutions
she placates the strain
tries vaguely to remember
between water and mirrors
which reflection inhabits her dreaming.

I

Ancient Offering

Over my neighbour's roof, the strange
light that artists love.
Darkness squats over trees
in a landscape bare of leaves
pauses in some skeletal
mime of movement.

Only my eyes are lanterns
observe ancient rites of propitiation.
Stately the Bacchae rise
up from their memoried deaths
bearing chants, cymbals and drums.

Against the backdrop of multiple fires turning
on many spits the haunches of those
which are rendered, Dionysian.

On the ground of an old year
the stains of drying
blood.

II

Modern Offering

In this time some remember Isis
in perverted rites
at Hallowe'en
open-toothed jack-o'-lantern leering
to please the spirits of the dead.

In this time
others pay tribute to vampires and ghouls
in theatres where darkness
pulls away their smiling.

Still others have learned to be
disarming, to turn rebellion
deep. Some buried waist high
in platitudes
raise the Christian god
on multiple crosses.

Candles cast red
on the walls of churches.
In this place, the Christian
need for ritual slaughter
evokes the edible god.

This is my flesh which is given you to eat.

Each December
Handel's triumphant "Messiah" drowns
out the horror that is our duplicate
and hungry flesh.
The Child
sacrificed by the Ancients
is grown to manhood
for the mute and makeshift cross.

Woman to the Second Power

She is all her limitations
shining in the grey
half-light of still another morning.

Desire is repeated on her limbs
hunger of lips and hands
seeking: the elusive
ideal of love.

Gaping like a wound
the scream that begins somewhere
the absence of anything but
a gnawing mockery of stars.

Daughter to men who want sons.
Worshipped and reviled
as madonna of the flowers
and whore
whose carnal name is never
long enough.

Receptacle for religious relics
tight pouch enclosing
dry seed, strange herbs.
Putrescent mother
bringing forth apocalyptic sons.

Death's second
she makes of birth and life itself
a mummery masquerading as gentle/
Woman.

Carried to the highest power
she is only the square root of female.

On the Stalk of Sometime

Agents of the king found her seated
eyes closed in a somnolent August.
At first they thought her hair
was full of birds
which rose in a flurry of wings
from the branches above her.
Feathered throats ricocheted
protest and raucous warning.

Slowly the queen raised
her eyelids. Irises
blue and thick as skin
enfolded the emissaries from the king.
Beneath the dandelion
heart of the sun
the couriers fell suddenly
and strangely adrift
seeds in a primordial harvest.

Then the queen offered her arm
to the captain of her husband's forces.
A net constructed
of legs and burly shoulders
the others closed around her.

At the exit to her garden she turned.
Her songbirds became ravens
black in the branches of blighted trees.
From the earth sprang
swords and skulls.
On the littered ground
shadows of scavengers, wheeling.

Her quiet eyes sent the captain
a story of lilies.
Suddenly words
were in the air around him
containing and enfolding
the seasons of carnage.
He shook away the image of antlers and blood
delivered her to the king
knowing that he had become
the rival of his sovereign.

Four A.M. Darkness

I

Outside this room
the air pounds in my temples
like an increase in density.

I pull to be lifted up.
Swing my searchlight
at the wreck of a wooden hulk.
From the depths
strange flattened fish burrow
in silt. I disturb them
with my incessant churning.

Unidentified
creatures scrape
against my face mask
and flutter.
Small currents radiate
from their fins like summer
heat on asphalt.

They pucker
and gulp pucker and gulp.
Sing me bizarre songs
from another element.
I kick and flounder
my finned legs.
Rise too fast.
My head fills with blood.
If I don't open my eyes
I shall die.

II

I wake curled around you
like a stream
following an embankment.
Scraping against my nighttime nerves
the dreams I carry.

In this four a.m. darkness
my hands trace you
wind walking on water:
thighs
belly
breasts.
Gathering love from your muscles
like tiger lilies.
Your skin pungent as cattails
at the swamp's edge:
scent of the loving we make.

With you beside me warm
I am on the rim of another precipice.
This plunge into living
like none I have taken
pulls at my fear.

Obituaries

My mother had huge ankles
and varicose veins.
She sang alto to my sister's soprano
rocking gently back and forth
arms linked across her bosom.
She wore her nylons rolled down
like socks
sitting with her legs apart
in a thin cotton dress.
She made a religion of poverty.
She was the embodied Pieta.

To this day I remember her belly
laugh. It shook her stomach
and vibrated my child's body
held in the folds of her fleshy arms.

My father on the contrary
was somber and thin
sweated profusely.
His skin was grey parchment
frown stitched in his forehead
like an old surgical scar
that would not heal.

He smelled of labour
overalls too large
and always dirty
from red brown fields.
His silence was dangerous
a prelude to fists smashed against wood
making plates rattle
teeth ache.

For a time it seemed he ground us
down like wheat in a flour mill
gathered us in sacks
where we could be stored
physically in corners.

My mother laughed and hummed
leaving to him
the punishment she thought
we justly deserved.
To him the strap
or willow branch
to her the role of encirclement
tentacles wrapping us close
to the smells of sex and dying.

All her life she was ill
and so a martyr.
All her life my father worked
like some bowed bewildered beast:
provider.
The message was clear to me
as traps sprung on the leg
of living: torment.

Love indeed binds, my parents'
voices sang
death is at the centre
of sex and we are guilty
of bringing you here to die.
Marry at your peril
and bear only if you do not
hear this song.

For years their lyrics
sucked in my veins
companion to aging.
Now I do not hear
the words when I open my thighs
to the heat of our desire.

But I still have their fear
of defeated passion
and the knowledge
that I too am dying.

Sins of the Fathers

I

My father. Against the early light he stood
in shadow swinging a double-bladed axe.
A silhouette in black
who bent and straightened
and bent again
knees trembling slightly.

The horses bent too
bellies to the ground
pulling at stumps
rooted in the earth:
coats glistening with the same
kind of sweat
same dusty rivulets
on their hides
as on my father's brow.
Sweat ran
from the tip of his nose
disorderly as tears
to the dust.

What the horses could not overturn
he again put to the axe:
bone-numbing repetitive strokes
until the roots finally gave.
He set brush fires
his throat burning in the afternoon
drank water for it
and spat.

By evening he was on the stone boat
bending, lifting
the stones his reward
for clearing the forest.
Behind him the sun glowed
red and violent.

Anxious he wrestled
to beat the darkness
approaching the time he could go in
and sleep
or make sons:
companions to this terrible labour.

II

My father has a brother whom he despises.
"He came out of the womb screaming
and he hasn't improved since,"
my father rumbles
"I had to look after him
I know what he's like.

"I got into rocking the cradle with my foot.
One time I knocked the cradle over
kicking too hard," he chuckles.
These many years later
he still savours his triumph
rubbing his palms on his pants.

"That bastard. I've seen him
cut the tail off a cow because she switched
him while he was milking."
Yes. And seen him
beat his horses with a two-by-four
because they couldn't haul
a granary through mud
to move it where he wanted.
"A man who mistreats animals
doesn't deserve to live."

My father warms to the reasons
for his indignation. "His sons are
just like him. I've seen them set
birds alight with kerosene
or taunt a bull tied to a post
until its nose bleeds
from trying to get loose."

He clears his throat and spits
a wisp of snuff
clinging to his bottom lip:
wipes it off with his sleeve.

My father and his brother:
both of them have very blue eyes.
Both make an incantation
of profanity
build their rages until
their eyes pale:
anger drawing them into ecstasy.
Rustling through them
like the wind through October leaves.
Anger stripping them bone bare.

III

My father and his detested brother.
I have seen them
racing each other to the bottom
of 26 ounces of Seagram's whiskey
tilting the empty
and crying over a sister they lost
years ago
arguing hoarsely over
what year she was born.

Neither of them mention
that they think their mother killed her
by packing off the child
and her husband's mistress
into the violence
of those early winters.

My grandmother did not come from France
to share her husband
divide a cabin
between two families
relate to a man
who would not renounce
his obligations to mistress or wife.

"It was a hard winter," my father says.
"There was frost on the walls
every morning
even though we kept a fire
overnight. Of course they died
a woman and a girl child.
They must have."

My uncle says nothing.
He reaches for the glass of whiskey
and drinks it neat
grimacing as acid overproof
courses through his blood.
"You're right Michel," he says.
"I was too small to remember
when Violette was born."
And he changes the topic
to the price of grain
and when to gather this year's
crop from the fields.

My father regards him
strangely, as if to say
how dare you admit you're wrong.

A Flower in the Desert

I

Who is this being
whose hair curls
springing tightly into existence
like sudden blossoms on hardy cacti
who is this being
with whom I am strangely
unutterably content.

She is still full
of frailties though ponderous
bearing the burden of husks
and harvest
winter and shorn fields
skin bursting like a granary.

Some of the fullness she clears
through her bowels
enjoying the orgasm of shitting

some of the fullness
is in her guts
recovered from the sacrificial
ground where she lay them

II

...this being like Sarah
hag of the desert
old flowering bush.
Her ovaries
for all too brief an instant
inspired by old seed
did Abraham the honour
of recreating him.

With ritual slaughter
he was willing to repay her.

III

Abraham she says now was full
of shit
he was willing to sacrifice
the son of our old age
for some absent god
who demanded too much
and was allowed to.

Old patriarch:
poking jealously at ovules
looking for signs
beyond this extraordinary flowering.

November Leaves

In this November
crystals of snow drift
harmless
spin away from contact with earth—
mix in pools of mud
ancient blending of compost and loam.

So many years and few
we watch November snatch
away the premises of spring.
Hear wind in the arteries
suck
begin the long escape from sap
running arrogance aground:
the assertion that life is
anything
other than seasonal.

Brittle resistance of bone and joint
ankles snapping
like those of the fragile
old—we see and glance
sharply away.

Houses penetrable
lowering skies
shapes like apparitions
real only when we sleep.

Peeling
of paint around windows loose
eavestroughing wood
rot ivy trailing towards
broken shingles.
                    More leaves trapped there.

So we believe in death and resurrection.
Christ or Buddha
extraterrestrials
or Superman.

There must be something.
Something greater
than raking leaves
lasting
beyond youth decrepitude
and this eclectic season.

A Memory for Worms

cestode words
parasitic when adult
in the intestine
of human and other
vertebrates:
tapeworms of the powerless
always-to-be-diminished
Self

mortality is after all
hearsay
evidence of numbers lost or
our own rate of failure

life originates
some of it from lifeless matter
abiogenesis
maggots grow out of the foraging
of flies out of our
soft-bellied grubbing

memory is legless
thick and lacking
in precision
whose one character is
a large capacity
for returning to former
conditions

we measure our cephalic index
by the maximum length
and breadth of a shrinking
skull
thought the premise upon which
fulfillment is denied

Sorry, I Don't Remember Your Name

You introduced yourself to me
by circling my nipples with your hands.
I said I love you
watched you recoil
the slow serpentine of your green eyes
changing.

You left abruptly.

I heard later that you had gone abroad
and had someone's baby
while healing the sick in Ecuador.
White Rhodesian expiating
the sins of your race collecting
the skins of third-world men.

Today on the street
quite by chance
you called to me.
I was startled into vagueness
by the naiads in your voice.
Emerald memories of a submerged city.

I said "I don't remember your name"—
the lie curling in my throat
like green bile.
Still I dare not hope
that now you are ready to love me.

The Barbs of Intention

Your labia intricate
complex: a world akin
to coral or fronds waving
in some underwater galaxy
clasping and letting swim
tiny fishes
currents of a clear unmenacing sea
flickering.

Lovers calcified float under coral
reefs compacted.
Trapped in the silt of many
years
I drift in some morass
crustacean fluctuate:
hiding.

Fear strand and net
haywire stray wire
rise
to catch a current larger
than intentions
refuse and shells.

Hemispheres

this morning you poise
with hands in pockets
face me
your eyes hidden behind glasses:
smile, careful to maintain
the proper distance between
two hemispheres.

motionless I reach for your mouth
as I would reach for water
tingling in the cold
shock of loving so
suddenly:
recall
your head burrowing
in the ridge
between my breasts
the wonderful eloquence
of your moving hands.

later you will open books
before me talk
about the high middle ages.
I trace the evolution of romanesque
in the curve of your mouth
sit on the back of the bronze
lion rearing towards the present
from centuries of art/
history.

Blight on the Evergreen

Pine needles rust-coloured
fall heavy on earth's belly
this summer of contradictions.
Ponderous rain rotted the berry crops
drought finds frogs breathing fast
sitting dull-eyed in mud.
Creek beds wrinkle
like ancient faces
or infants too long in wombs.

One day you take a watering can to the woodpile
revive a garter snake
dehydrating in the sun.
We find his cousin dead in the roadside
six inches from the pond
stand over stagnant water which reflects us.

The squash flourishing with our care
stirs in the breeze
orange flowers open-mouthed.

Perennials

Summer days are growing longer
crab grass and weeds
on our front lawn
menace like the memory of scissors.

In the garden you weed and trowel
smudge your brow
with honest dirt:
honest as you are.
Your trying catches at my throat.

Shall we find it buried in the earth?
that tenacious friendship
that quickens still
so much between us
underground.

Some seeds germinate
slowly
and become perennials
outlasting the cruelties of frost
and declining sun:
seedlings that are believed lost
like hope or childhood
you the sturdiest
slow starter
you who do not want to finish.

Your roots go deeper than you know.

Lynn Valley Canyon: Summer 1981

We flirt on the edge of at least two worlds
—spans across a foaming canyon.
Forth and back
over a rope bridge swaying—
small and blanketed
in fine mist:
precursors of eternity or nothingness.

We do not pursue
the many holes that runnel rock
habits blunt as granite
resistant to one another.

Carved from an outcropping of rock
the visage of a woman
grief dripping from her stone face.
Her hair a clump of green
springing dishevelled
from her anxious brow

plumed hat a tree
growing from her brain
by the roots.
Tears leaking from her blind eyes
into a wild gathering.

On this tenuous bridge
adolescents lunge
jeering as we scramble
away from precipitate death.
Their mad plunging
shakes our hold on living.

When they have gone
the bridge is still. I do not want
to see your eyes
or check the more eternal
face of sorrow.

Love and flesh are fragile.
Our fear of losing both
keeps us here
balancing.

Festival (Home County Truce)

In this afternoon of my grieving
the sun beats
a bagpipe more beautiful than usual
skreals
someone with a thin flute
someone else with large bongos
keeps time.

Sun reddens
the faces of those who listen:
shimmers in this July
the heat rising
like amplified sound.

Sadness does not belong
at the zenith of summer
with a new love chosen
and preferred beside me.
Let me relinquish.
Lay you to rest
my past lover
who is so hard to leave.

Beneath the skirted statue
here in Victoria Park
blue metal offering
perpetual flowers
to soldiers dead and gone
I am seated.
A grisly brown tank
is parked incongruously
among thousands of celebrants
many of us younger
than the War.
Our lives run forward
the future mortal in each cell.

We make music
feast and join our bodies
in the scattered circles
of our dying.

Riding the Bus

Riding the bus
like riding the elevator
is an exercise in not being numb.

These September mornings
students press on either side
equipped with duffel bags
and notice-me expressions.

They could all model for Calvin Klein.
In their half-formulated faces
the hint of adult rigidities:
cosmetic masks
uniform styles
address their fear of being
different.
Puppets jump behind their
nervous teeth.

The boys learning to be men
who are not soft. The girls
learning to be women who
are not soft either.
Growing up on video games
which parody the death
of this and every other planet.

The elderly too are making
an early start of it.
Trying to get the jump on bargains
at glossy department stores.
Too old not to be
part of 9 to 5.

Umbrellas
built before the collapsible era
draped through the handles
of bottomless purses.
Limbs composed of stout
canes and serviceable black shoes.

Sometimes
ancient eyes glare
angry at the young
offender who, seated, ignores
their infirmities.

Sometimes
moral outrage is as subtle as an
indrawn breath:
is everyone's companion
on a crowded bus.
Our routines and our fears choking us.

Shattered Glass

I am obligated to dictionaries
for helping me explain
what shattered glass approximates:
that which is
damaged or altered
that which has
separated into parts, violently;
that which has undergone
or been subjected to fracture.

One looks vainly for patterns
for ways of piecing together
that which has been:
intelligence is made bankrupt
by the incomplete.

I have been gathering
jagged pieces for weeks now.
Fragments gleam in the carpet
teach my feet
the value of foresight.

Eden: 1982

Sometimes all is not well
in the garden of Eden.
The snake writhes somewhere between sheets of palm
leaves draped over sun-ripe figs
destined for consumption.

Hold them in your hands
figs soft as the promise of nipples.
Raise them for the eating
sun bursting from inside
plump round skins:
bursting from inside
like my slow reluctant ways.

Sometimes one may suppose
that all is well in Eden.
Beyond our skins the birds join:
a chorus of praise
piety simple as fat worms
shaken in the beak
small dance of claws and wings
on the stirring grass.

In my throat love flows
sweet song in this oriole breast
pastoral contradictions
in an ancient garden.
Foreground: the idyll of figs and snakes
doubling.

Twining around your life
I may bring coils
silence hissing in the dark
my self-containment.
Doubt
with its dark leaves
stirring.

Still the memory of figs
fills my mouth.

And Still the Sun

I

And still the sun shimmers
on green leaves the wind caresses
flowers sprawl bold
fragile lovely.

In the garden
corn stirs
far removed from silver tassels
or even the beginning of husks.
My tomato plants
stretch their long dark leaves
outward to the sun. Still
there is no fruit, nor even the flower
to presage bearing.

In a room over the garden
you draw me
softly with your hands
inside my warm skin. I am taut
ripe and full. It is not the season.

I am roots growing
down deep digging in the earth
out of which I came
from which I have lived
in exile
narrow furrows neat rows
tendrils clinging only
to some shallow
cleft.

In this rare moment
the sun finds us
streaming through the glass.
We are present
lifted out of time
and in it, full.

II

Suddenly the breeze flattens
lengthening like the withers
of a galloping horse, belly
close to the ground
hooves rattling
across the eaves.
Long slashes of heat
illuminate neighbouring roofs.
Whickering nostrils
red eye of the storm.
Its blackened teeth.

White stones
slash at the windows
gather in icy runnels
on every ledge.
The neighbour's tabbies run frantic
between window and door
a mother whose two kittens follow her.
No one answers their calls
their scratches and entreaties.
The frail windows remain closed.

Across from their roof
we run to close up
put out buckets and pots
to contain an avalanche of rain.
My plants bend. Dill flattens.
Butter lettuce sags.

It is not fair: to plant and thin
and weed and not to harvest.
Hunkering down where the ground
is a flattened green sea
running mud and rippling.

After the storm
what is left is anger
and the edge of a thin fear.

This Is My Beloved Dyke

This is my beloved dyke
in whom I am well pleased.
She leadeth me to green pastures
she lies down beside me
daisies and black-eyed
susans adorn her hair.

She is Adam's rib
rising from his ennui
his Eve-you-did-it-all
you-dragged-me-down
cunt
to claim her own pleasure:
clear geyser breaking
from the ground
flight of pigeons or of doves
symmetry of pelvic bone.

She is leisure stretched upon the earth
thighs aching with woman love—
laughter
beating in the blood
like birth.

She is every window you have
ever glanced through
every mirror casting back
reflections.

Artemis is moonlight
Acteon slain
she stands
legs pausing
between yesterday and never.

Jesus freezes
on instant replay.
Billy Graham goes to bat
for the Chicago Red Socks.
The moon hangs on a narrow thread
leering.

All things are as they should be.
She takes me
today she takes me.

I am chosen to carry fishes
from Galilee.

A Gift of Pearls

The moon is full
lapping up the light from Venus
brilliant in the dawn.

Clouds obscure it
then race away like veils
revealing the body of Salome.

This morning your face in sleep
gentles and excites:
I reach for your thighs
as though I am waves
lapping
lapping
and you under water.

Half-open oyster
where seaweed and sand reach
entangle my hand
protect the pearl I never dare
tell you about
although I speak of oysters.

Not perfect nor round nor even
the same milky shade
you turn within my hand
seek my throat
to hang there
invisible pendant of growing
to know the seasons of pearl.

You lie
languid shell
protecting from the jaws
of predators your soft
your edible core
while I seek you out
tongue tasting your delicate salt
licking of waves
lapping of tides.

You will say love:
wake to the smells of me
in your hair
and the sounds
the sounds
of oysters beaching.

Prisms

Sometimes your smile is
reflected in millions of prisms
small worlds of colour.

Under the street lamps
rimmed with aureoles
the morning flutters:
unseen birds utter
rills to the goddess of dawn.
                        My own throat fills.

Times like these
I am my skin
edible as olives:
am
trees and grass and quavering song
permutations of molecule and form.

Should I define the feasible
the doors to morning
will close
the world become
a place of trimmed hedges
and streets falling linear
in four directions.

For now this moment
hangs, a pendulum of possibilities.
It catches and reflects light.

Wordless you sit beside me
on the porch.

If you enjoyed *The Square Root of Female,* you might wish to read other Ragweed titles in our ongoing series of women's books. Ragweed Press publishes fine books by women! Other books in our series are:

Poetry and Fiction

Binding Twine 0-920304-32-X $8.95
Penny Kemp
A series of interrelated poems about the excruciating, unthinkable ordeal of the author losing custody of her children.

The Book of Fears 0-920304-31-1 $8.95
Susan Kerslake
Short stories with a strange, subterranean beauty about the vast landscape of fear.

Island Women: Prose and Poetry 0-920304-19-2 $5.50
An anthology of work by 49 Island women prepared for the Island Women's Arts Festival.

Out On The Plain 0-920304-37-0 $7.95
Frankie Finn
This first novel breaks exciting new ground, developing links between four women while destroying the conventional barriers between the author and her characters, and between the reader and the novel itself.

Susan: More Running in the Wind Stories 0-920304-22-2 $5.95
Olive O'Brien
Delightful recollections of growing up on an Island farm in the early 1900s.

Young People

The Private Adventures of Brupp 0-920304-25-7 $4.95
Deirdre Kessler
Brupp is an extraordinary cat who keeps an imaginary diary. He sets off to see the world from an Island farm. Nine volumes in the series for the nine lives of Brupp. Second volume due October 1984.

The Witch of Port LaJoye 0-920304-29-5 $8.95
Joyce Barkhouse
A haunting legend of a young Basque girl who learns the healing ways of the Micmac, only to be called a witch by the settlers and burned at the stake.

Available (we hope!) at your local bookstore. Or send cheque or money order to Ragweed Press, Box 2023, Charlottetown, P. E. I. C1A 7N7 (include 50 cents for postage).